ANIMALS

BY KEV PAYNE

DK

CONTENTS

TERRIBLY TOXIC

Some dangerous animals are poisonous and some are venomous. Poison gets into the body by being swallowed, inhaled, or absorbed. Venom is injected by animals through bites, spines, or stings. Either way, both can be deadly, so other animals better beware!

Blistering beetles

Blister beetles get their name from the poisonous chemicals they release, which cause painful swelling and blistering of the skin. It can take over a week for the blisters to heal. Horses sometimes eat the beetles while feeding on hay and get a nasty surprise.

Best of both

Although rare, there are species that can be both venomous and poisonous at the same time. Tiger keelback snakes from Japan are armed with a venomous bite, but they also become poisonous from the toxic toads that they eat.

Death dealers

Deathstalker scorpions are some of the deadliest scorpions in the world. They hide under rocks to wait for an unsuspecting victim, such as a cricket, to walk by. They grab the cricket with their pincers before quickly stinging it with their tails. With the cricket paralyzed or dead, the scorpions are free to enjoy their meal.

Frightening frogs

The bright colours of poison dart frogs found in South America show how deadly they are. The skin of the golden poison dartfrog is coated in a lethal toxin, which causes paralysis and death. They are considered one of the most toxic animals on Earth. Despite never growing bigger than the size of a chicken's egg, one frog has enough poison to kill 10 people. In the past, the strong poison was also used by hunters in Colombia who rubbed the tips of their arrows along the backs of the frogs.

Do you mind?

SUPER SLIMERS

Do you enjoy making slime? Do you wish you could have a never-ending supply? Well come and meet the animals that can – the super slimers!

Dinner is served!

Butt butter

Hyenas produce a slime that is also known as "hyena butter". But before you grab a knife to spread it on your toast, remember that the substance is produced in glands in the hyena's bottom. The hyenas share the "butter" by rubbing their butts against trees and rocks. It is believed that they do this to mark their territory.

Shut your mouth!

Found in the United States, the slimy salamander, as the name suggests, is known for producing a sticky, glue-like slime that is difficult to remove. With just a flick of the salamander's tail, any predators who come across the substance may find that they can no longer move their mouths!

Bye!

Opossums, small marsupials native to the United States, are slimy tricksters. When faced with attackers, they will lie on the ground for hours and pretend to be dead. They will also make themselves less appealing by pooing out a green, foul-smelling slime. Hopefully their acting doesn't stink, too!

Slime superstar!

Hagfish, which are eel-like animals, are slime superstars. When attacked, hagfish release up to 1 litre (nearly 2 pints) of gooey slime into the predator's face – that's about as much as six full glasses. This makes it difficult for the predator to breathe. A hagfish can use this on prey much larger than itself – such as a shark. The slime mixes with salt water and quickly expands to create huge amounts of clear goo. The fibres in the slime are so incredibly strong, it could even be used to create clothing – including bullet-proof vests!

RECORD BREAKERS

While gaining a gold medal might be the peak of an athlete's career, here are some world records that very few would be proud of.

Smelliest

Although many animals are up for the title, the African zorilla is considered one of the smelliest animals on Earth. When threatened, they will raise their tails and growl or bark. If this doesn't work, they will spin round and spray yellow liquid from stink glands in their bottoms. This temporarily blinds their enemy. The smell is so strong, it can help zorillas to defend themselves against lions.

Largest amount of poo

With the blue whale being the world's biggest animal, it makes sense that it also creates the most poo. The animal can produce up to 200 litres (350 pints) of poo in one go – that's around three wheelbarrows! The poo itself is said to smell like dog poo, but it has the consistency of breadcrumbs.

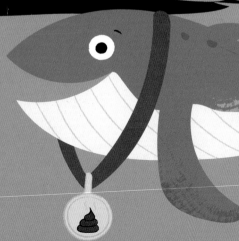

Most toxic

Living mainly in the waters of Australia and the Indo Pacific, box jellyfish are one of the most toxic animals on Earth. The venom they produce attacks the heart, nervous system, and skin cells of any creature that encounters it. Box jellyfish are each armed with 5,000 stinging cells. They also have 24 eyes, one of which is always looking up, even if it's swimming upside down.

A blue whale's heart weighs around 180 kilograms (28 stone) and is the same size as a dodgem!

BEASTLY BABIES

The animal kingdom is filled with all kinds of babies. On these pages, discover all the doting dads, magnificent mums, and the truly beastly babies!

Tiger sharks eat almost anything – including rubbish!

Baby shark

Tiger sharks learn to be deadly even before they are born. While still in the womb, the babies will fight, kill, and eat each other. Despite carrying hundreds of eggs, only one or two victorious sharks will be born.

Daddy love

Found in Chile and Argentina, male Darwin's frogs will watch closely when the female lays eggs. Once they turn into tadpoles, the father will swallow them, storing them within his vocal sac. When the tadpoles turn into froglets they will emerge from his mouth.

Yummy mummy!

All parents care for their young but female velvet spiders take things to the next level. Not only will the mother spider regurgitate food to feed her babies, but she will also allow them to nibble on her.

Top of the pops!

Found mainly in South America, the male Surinam toad, after mating, will push dozens of fertilized eggs onto the female's back, where they will stick to her skin. Her skin grows over the eggs until they are completely covered. After three to four months, the toadlets will pop out of the mother's back, ready to look for food – often this means each other!

BLUE-RINGED OCTOPUS

Blue-ringed octopuses, found in the shallow waters around Australia and Japan, are one of the most venomous creatures in the ocean. They feed on fish and small crustaceans, such as shrimp and crab. They have toxic saliva that stuns the prey and a powerful bite that can crack through the victims shell.

Deadly

Despite its small size, the blue-ringed octopus holds enough venom to kill 26 adults in a matter of minutes. There is no known antidote.

Watch out!

Egg danger

The bacteria that produces the toxic saliva are passed on to the octopus's young so even their eggs are ready with venom.

Name:
Blue-ringed octopus

Nickname: Bro

Place of Origin:
Japan and Australia

Size: 20–25 centimetres
(8–10 inches)

Party time!

Disco dazzler

Blue-ringed octopuses have bright blue rings all over their bodies, which pulsate as a warning to other animals. When threatened, more than 50 rings flash in a third of a second to produce a dazzling display.

FIERCE FIGHTERS

Animals fight for a variety of reasons. While some battle for control, for food, or for a mate, others just fight for their lives. Punching, kicking, biting – these fierce fighters will do all they can to win!

Air force

Beaded lacewing larvae attack termites with farts. They will use their toxic gas to stun six termites in one blast so they can feast on the paralyzed victims.

Kick back

Zebras are prey to a number of predators, including cheetahs, lions, and crocodiles. To try and survive, they will defend themselves, and their herds, by biting, pushing, and kicking. It is the kick that is the most lethal and is powerful enough to break skulls – which can even cause instant death to an attacker.

Fast food

The fastest land animal on Earth, cheetahs are also fierce fighters. They use their incredible speeds to knock over prey, such as rabbits, warthogs, and gazelles, before delivering a fatal attack to the throat.

FUNKY FARTS

It's not just humans that fart. All animals that have intestines find that air is released at some point. So the next time you decide to drop a "botty burp" why not try pinning the blame on a passing dog, cow, or even a termite!

Some seals can hold their breath for up to two hours – particularly useful if someone's farted!

World's worst?

People who work with seals and sea lions have suggested that the title of "World's Stinkiest Farts" should belong to these marine mammals. The pungent smell described may be down to their diet of fish and squid.

Living in shallow pools in Mexico, the Bolson pupfish will feed on algae, and sometimes slurp up the gas bubbles released by the algae, too. The extra gas can cause the fish to become bloated and float to the surface of the water – making them easy targets for predators. So, to save themselves, they fart. If they don't do this in time, there is also a chance they will explode!

Are those bubbles coming from you?

Smelephants

Elephant farts are particularly bad! In zoos, keepers feed them a special "fart fighting" diet. The magical "antidote" includes rice and garlic.

17

POO POWER!

Whether it's marking an animal's territory, for protection, or even as a tasty snack, the power of poo knows no bounds!

What a hit!

Found in the United States, the tortoise beetle larvae use their poo as a shield. The creature dabs poo onto the end of a fork that sticks out of its bottom, and then hits ants and beetles with it to avoid being eaten. Smashing idea!

Shoot the poo

Some predators are weirdly attracted to the smell of caterpillar poo! To avoid being eaten, caterpillars shoot poo out of their bottoms and fling it as far away as possible. It can be thrown distances of up to 40 times their own body length, the same as you kicking a rugby ball across a pitch – normally 70 metres (230 feet). Talk about putting them off the scent!

See ya!

Start with poo

Forget milk – at six months old, baby koalas will tuck into a hearty meal of their mother's poo, direct from her bottom. The mother produces a runny substance called "pap". The pap contains nutrients and helpful bacteria from the mother's gut that will help the baby as it grows.

That's better!

Hot to trots

Feeling hot? Several species of birds choose to cool down by pooing on their own feet. The evaporation of poo and wee cools them down. However too much of this special "sun cream" can lead to the legs becoming sore.

ZOMBIE ATTACK!

A zombie is a mythological creature, a dead person brought back to life. Films love to show zombies walking as if in a trance, searching for brains to eat, but in the animal kingdom this may not be too far from the truth.

BINS!

Trash zombies

In 2019 in the United States, police warned people to watch out for "zombie raccoons" who had been seen staggering around with glowing eyes and showing their sharp teeth. Their abnormal behaviour was caused by a viral disease called "distemper".

If a carpenter ant accidentally inhales the spores of a mind-controlling fungus, it will find itself behaving rather strangely. As if in a trance, the infected ant will leave the ant colony (group) and climb to a higher position, where it will stay. Eventually, the fungus will burst through the ant's body releasing more spores that will shower down upon other members of the colony below.

Yay! It's snowing!

Deer, oh deer

"Zombie deer disease" is a deadly infection that causes animals, such as deer and moose, to lose weight, drool, and become less scared of humans.

MONKEY BUSINESS

There are more than 260 species of monkey, and some of them sure can be cheeky! Will these tricksters ever stop monkeying around?

Fat chance

"Uncle Fat" was the name given to a very overweight macaque in Thailand. He got the nickname because he was eating so much junk food, which had been left behind by tourists. As leader of his pack, he would also get other monkeys to bring food to him. "Uncle Fat" is now on a strict diet of lean protein, fruit, and vegetables to help him lose weight.

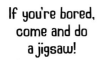

If you're bored, come and do a jigsaw!

Fab flingers

Some monkeys have been known to throw poo in zoos. While some zoologists believe it is because they are angry or stressed, some think it may be a sign of boredom.

Bright bums

Happy new rear!

Male mandrills have bright, colourful bottoms, the brightest belonging to the leader of the group. If, however, another male defeats him in a fight, the victor's bottom will become brighter as he becomes the new leader.

Pee perfume

To attract a mate, male capuchin monkeys will wee on their hands and then rub it into their fur.

GREATER SHORT-HORNED LIZARD

Greater short-horned lizards have wide, flat bodies covered in short horns. They look like "horned toads", but they are reptiles, not amphibians. Their small size and colour, which matches the soil where they live, camouflages them.

Slimy snack

The lizard's main source of food is ants, including the venomous harvester ant. To avoid being stung, the lizard doesn't crunch the ant. After catching an ant with its sticky tongue, the lizard wraps it in slime and swallows it whole.

Name:
Greater short-horned lizard

Nickname: Horned toad

Place of Origin:
North and Central America

Size: 6–15 centimetres
(2–6 inches)

Stop or I'll shoot!

Despite their numerous horns, the lizards are prey to a number of predators. To try and ward them off, they will inflate their bodies to twice their size and shoot blood from the corners of their eyes.

Yuck!

The blood can squirt up to 1 metre (3 feet) and is meant to confuse attackers. It also contains a foul-tasting chemical that is harmful to some animals.

YUCKY MAMMALS

Whales, bears, jaguars, foxes, and humans
– there are more than 5,000 species of
mammals found all over the world.
But beware – some of them have
horrible habits!

The deadly bite

Slow lorises are found in southeast Asia and are the world's only venomous primate. When threatened, they produce a toxic liquid from glands near their elbows and then raise their arms over their heads, while hissing. They lick up the venom and spread it onto their teeth – ready to deliver a toxic bite.

Hey! I'm the king!

No, I am!

I'm the king!

Unlike in fairy tales where a rat king rules as the largest rodent of a group, with big muscles and a crown, a real rat king is far more gross. A rat king happens when the tails of a group of rats become twisted and tangled into a knot that cannot be undone.

Superstore

Moles are very fond of worms and store them in special underground chambers. Moles eat 60 per cent of their body weight in worms each day, which may explain why one chamber has been found filled with 370 worms! To stop the worms from wriggling away, the moles will bite them on the back of the head so they can't escape while still keeping fresh and tasty.

RADICAL REPTILES

Snakes, crocodiles, turtles, and lizards are all reptiles. Snakes and lizards smell with their tongues – by picking up tiny chemical particles in the air. At least we can choose to hold our noses if we smell a pair of stinky socks. Imagine having to use your tongue!

A rhombic egg eater's mouth is lined with little ridges that are similar to human fingerprints.

Jaw dropping

Rhombic egg-eating snakes are mainly found in southern Africa. They have very flexible jaws that allow them to swallow eggs whole. Once the egg is inside its mouth, the snake squeezes its muscles and cracks the shell, allowing it to swallow the liquid inside. It then spits the eggshell out. Talk about biting off more than you can chew!

Live to tell the tail

An excited dog will wag its tail but geckos wave theirs for a different reason. When threatened by a predator, a gecko will wag its tail to encourage the predator to attack it. If it does, the gecko will quickly snap off its tail, leaving it free to escape. Don't panic – its tail can grow back!

Phew!

Getting ahead

Native to Australia, thorny dragons are reptiles with plenty of tricks to help them avoid being eaten. As well as being covered in hard, sharp spikes, thorny dragons have false heads on their shoulders. When threatened, the creatures will dip their real head and use the fake head to confuse the predator. They can also inflate their chests to make themselves bigger and harder to swallow.

BIRD BEHAVIOUR

There are around 10,000 species of birds in the world. Most birds can fly – although not all. Many can also jump, swim, dive, and run.

Big mouth

Pelicans are large birds with pouches in their throat called "gulars". These pouches can hold even more than their bellies can. Pelicans will scoop up water to catch fish and then drain the water before swallowing the fish whole and alive. Pelicans have also been seen eating seagulls and turtles.

Dinner is served

Shrikes are a family of small songbirds that are not as innocent as they seem. They are fierce predators and will tackle prey the same size as them. They will impale larger prey, like mice or lizards, on sharp thorns.

Hoatzins are tropical birds found in South America. They are known as "stink birds". Hoatzins are said to smell like cow manure and this is caused by the fact that they eat leaves and flowers that rot in their digestive system.

Be wary of cassowary

The most deadly bird to humans is thought to be the cassowary, a large bird found in the tropical forests of southeast Asia and Australia. Cassowaries have sharp claws and powerful legs – for delivering strong kicks. Although rare,if they kick a human it can be deadly.

AWFUL AMPHIBIANS

There are more than 4,000 species of amphibian, including toads, frogs, and salamanders. They live partly in water and partly on land. Talk about multitasking!

Brrr-ribbit

Wood frog tadpoles eat algae, eggs... and each other!

Found across northern America, wood frogs will partially freeze when it gets really cold. Ice crystals can form under their skin and in their body, yet they do not die. This is because their main organs are surrounded with substances that stop them from freezing. Though they may stop breathing and their heart may stop beating, once the temperatures rise the frogs are ready to get hopping again!

You'll do anything to get out of the washing up!

Watch your step

If you've ever stepped in chewing gum then you may know a little about how it feels to be a tree frog. Tree frogs release sticky slime from pads in their feet, which helps them to cling on to trees and leaves. Special channels in their feet wipe away dirt so that they can produce a clean batch of slime with each new step.

Is dinner ready?

Olms are salamanders that live in dark caves in Europe. Though nearly blind, they have a very good sense of taste, smell, and hearing. They swim like eels and swallow their prey whole. Since they eat so much food in one go, olms can survive for up to 10 years without eating again!

I'm hungry.

But you only ate six years ago!

DUNG BEETLE

While we try to avoid animal droppings, dung beetles, as their name suggests, can't get enough! Most dung beetles rely on the droppings of herbivores (animals that only eat plants), as their poo contains undigested grass and smelly liquid. If a poo is too dry, then the beetles can't suck out the nutrients they need.

Dung babies

Dung beetles lay their eggs in poo so that their babies can start eating as soon as they hatch.

Super strong!

Despite their small size, dung beetles are incredibly strong and can lift balls of poo 50 times their own body weight. In relation to its size, the dung beetle is the world's strongest animal.

Poo and away!

Although they spend a lot of time on the ground, dung beetles do have wings and can fly several miles in search of the perfect poo.

Name: Dung beetle

Nickname: Tumblebug

Place of Origin: Everywhere except Antarctica

Size: 1.3–6.3 centimetres (0.5–2.5 inches)

ICKY INSECTS

Although tiny, there are more species of insect than any other group on the planet. There are also lots of them – it is thought that for every human on Earth there are 1.4 billion insects.

No! The fridge is this way, dummy!

Headless hunters

Cockroaches can survive for weeks without their heads. This is because they don't breathe like we do – they use holes called spiracles all over their bodies. They will die eventually, however, as they are unable to eat or drink.

Bombs away!

Bombadier beetles release chemical stink bombs from their rear ends. The liquid they squirt out is strong enough to burn human skin. Their explosions can even save their lives when they've been swallowed by frogs, who will throw up the beetles as soon as they taste the foul liquid.

You suck!

After sucking their ant victims dry, assassin bugs stack the bodies on their backs to warn off predators.

Head start

The gum leaf skeletoniser is a tiny caterpillar found in Australia. It has two nicknames – the "unicorn caterpillar" and the "mad hatterpillar", which relate to something it does as it grows. When the caterpillar gets bigger and moults, it will stack its own empty head casings upon its real head to create a horn. It can do this up to 13 times before it transforms into a moth! It is believed that the extra heads give some form of protection from predators, confusing them during an attack.

FOUL FISH

There are more than 30,000 known species of fish, with new ones being found every year. Fossil records suggest fish have been on Earth for more than half a million years.

Say ahhh!

Veggie vampires

Pacu fish are found in South America and are sometimes referred to as "vegetarian piranhas". Unlike the piranha, a pacu's diet mainly consists of plants, algae, and fruits, although it will also eat smaller fish. Pacus have teeth similar to humans and use them to help crack nuts and grind down plants.

Deadly delicacy

When threatened, puffer fish will inflate themselves full of water, nearly doubling in size. This makes it more difficult for potential predators to bite them. However, they also have toxins strong enough to kill 30 humans. Despite being poisonous, the fish is considered a delicacy to eat in Japan.

Feeding Frenzy

A fish with the fiercest of reputations is the piranha. These South American fish have round bodies, large heads, and razor-sharp teeth. The red-bellied piranha has sharper teeth and stronger jaws than any other species. They hunt in groups and come together in a feeding frenzy to feast on large animals. Their attacks are so brutal that an animal can be stripped of its flesh in minutes.

Bubble blowers

Have you ever blown a spit bubble? How about one with an egg in it? That is what many species of fish do. After the eggs are released, parents will gather them into their mouths and then blow them back out in a nest of bubbles covered in mucus. The nest will then float to the surface of the water and stay there until the fish hatch.

They blow up so fast!

UP IN THE SKY

It's not only birds that can navigate through the air – there are many species of animal that can take to the skies. These include snakes, squirrels, and even creatures that live in the sea!

Flying high

Draco lizards live among the trees of southeast Asia, safe from the predators that prowl the forest floor. Folds of skin between their ribs act as wings, helping the lizards to glide from tree to tree. They use their long tails to steer themselves.

Hairy paper!

Colugos live in the tropical rainforests of southeast Asia and spend most of their days clinging to trees. They have a fur-covered membrane that goes from their face to their tail. When stretched out, this makes them look like a hairy sheet of paper. The membrane helps them to catch the wind so that they can glide from trunk to trunk.

During his famous voyage on the *HMS Beagle*, Charles Darwin reported seeing flying spiders on the deck of the ship!

Ballooning spiders

Even though spiders don't have wings, this doesn't stop them from taking to the air. To fly, they will climb to a high point, raise their stomachs in the air, and produce a few strands of silk before being whisked away. They have been spotted more than 3.2 kilometres (2 miles) up in the air and 16,000 kilometres (around 9,950 miles) out to sea.

HIDDEN DEPTHS

A whole other world exists below the surface.
Dive into the murky ocean depths or unearth the
soil to discover the creatures that live there.

Devil down deep

The title of deepest-living land
animal on Earth currently goes to
the "devil worm". Discovered more
than 3 kilometres (nearly 2 miles)
down in the depths of a South
African gold mine, the worms
have adapted to living under
extreme pressure and heat.

Butt of the joke

Sea cucumbers are ocean-dwelling creatures that have long
bodies, leathery skin, and a multi-functional bottom. When
threatened, they will shoot out their internal organs and then
grow new ones. They also breathe through their bottoms.
Sometimes, small fish will live in their bottoms, too! They have
been known to eat the sea cucumbers from the inside out.

NO
VACANCIES

Slimy sea slugs

Nudibranchs are slime-oozing sea slugs that live in tropical waters. They are found in a variety of bright colours, which can give you a hint as to what they have been eating. When feeding, a nudibranch will absorb and display the colours of its prey.

> Well, *somebody* ate all the chocolates!

Sink or swim

You may have used armbands to help you swim but manatees use something entirely different – their farts. By releasing and storing their gas, the manatees can control how they sink or float in the water. If they want to float to the surface, they've got to hold their farts in, but if they want to get down deep they've just got to let it rip.

> You could have warned me!

PLENTY MORE POO

There's no escaping the fact that all animals poo.
Due to the large amounts of poo, animals have
developed some very interesting ways of
dealing with it!

Pink poo

Adélie penguins, that live across Antarctica,
are very fond of eating krill, a tiny pink crustacean.
They eat so much of it that it turns their poo pink.
The poo stains everything, including the ground
and the penguins' bodies. The pink poo
is so bright that it can even be seen
from space!

Although small, Adélie
penguins are brave and will
take on larger predators
than themselves, like seals.

Eggcellent idea

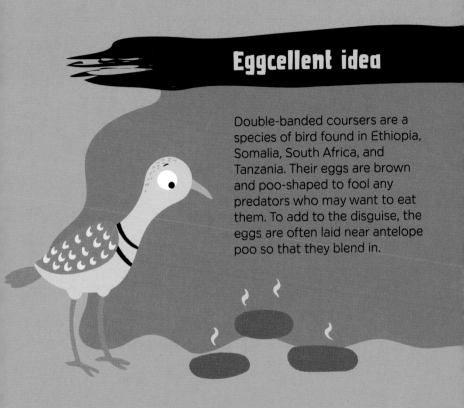

Double-banded coursers are a species of bird found in Ethiopia, Somalia, South Africa, and Tanzania. Their eggs are brown and poo-shaped to fool any predators who may want to eat them. To add to the disguise, the eggs are often laid near antelope poo so that they blend in.

One lump or two?

Native to Australia, wombats are the only animals in the world that produce cube-shaped poo. Their intestines shape the poo as it travels through the gut. Some scientists believe that the shape means the poo won't easily roll away and this helps the wombats mark out their territory.

HONEY BADGER

Honey badgers get their name from their love of feeding on honey and honey bee larvae. Their bites are strong enough to crack through a tortoise shell. These badgers are immune to venom, which means that they can eat scorpions and snakes without any trouble.

Tool tacklers

Honey badgers are intelligent creatures. They are one of the few species, other than primates, that can use tools. In captivity, they have been seen working together to unlock gates.

Super stink

Under their tails are special glands that can squirt out a foul-smelling liquid to help the honey badgers defend themselves. The strong smell can be detected up to 40 metres (130 feet) away – that's nearly the same distance as the width of a football pitch!

Name:
Honey badger

Nickname: Ratel

Place of Origin:
Africa, the Middle East, and India

Size: 70–100 centimetres (27–40 inches)

Watch out!

Honey badgers have a ferocious temper and can take on animals that are much bigger in size, such as lions and antelope.

Okay, okay! I'm backing up!

CREEPY CRITTERS

Goblins, vampires, monsters, and yetis – sounds like something from a horror story. But in the world of animals you don't need to wait until Halloween to meet them – they're among us now.

The monster

One of only two venomous lizards in the world, Gila monsters get their name from the Gila River basin, in the United States, where they were first discovered. While other creatures may inject venom through a sting, Gila monsters bite their victims, hold on, and chew. Currently, there is no antivenom to these bites, so stay away from these crafty creatures!

The yeti

First discovered in 2005, yeti crabs get their name due to their hairy arms, which give them a look similar to the mythical abominable snowman. Yeti crabs live on the ocean floor, close to vents that spew out boiling hot water. Their main source of food is bacteria that grows on their hairy arms.

The goblin

Goblin sharks live at the bottom of the ocean. They have a snout that sticks out from their head and extendable jaws. These jaws can shoot out to catch prey that is just out of reach.

Just...
a little...
further.

The vampire

Despite what they are called, vampire squid are not vampires. Their name comes from their dark red colouring and the flaps of skin between their tentacles that look like a vampire's swishing cape. When frightened, vampire squid will squirt clouds of blue, glowing mucus into the water to confuse predators.

No, you suck!

PRAYING MANTIS

The praying mantis gets its name from the position of its forelegs, which look like they are deep in prayer. These front legs also have sharp spines on them, which help clamp on to and capture prey. They have super-fast reactions that mean they can quickly skewer their arms into insects, before biting off their head to them from escaping.

All eyes on you

These insects have five eyes and can turn their head 180 degrees so that they can scan their surroundings. They have two eyes at the sides to detect movement and light, and three eyes in the middle to see. Praying mantises also just have one ear, which is on their belly.

Name:
Praying mantis

Nickname: Devil's horse,
Mule killer

Place of Origin:
North America, South
America, Europe, Africa, Asia,
and Australasia

Size: 1–15 centimetres
(0.4–6 inches)

Fast and Ferocious!

Praying mantises use their colour
to camouflage in vegetation.
This helps them avoid predators
and to ambush prey. They are
ferocious predators. They are even
known to eat hummingbirds if
they venture too close in search
of sugary water from plants.

KAPOW!

Adaptation is important for survival in the animal kingdom. Some animals have adapted special features that allow them to fight off predators and transform in the blink of an eye!

Sure shot

Can you pop a bubble with a noise that's louder than a gunshot? A pistol shrimp can! These small creatures have two claws, the larger of which is used to pop bubbles with such pressure that its prey can die from the shockwave instantly. They are so noisy that pistol shrimps were even used in World War II to mask submarine noises!

I'm armed!

Only ribbing

Spanish ribbed newts get their name from the way they defend themselves from predators. When threatened, their sharp ribs poke out through their sides. Not only does this make them more difficult to eat, but a toxin that covers the ribs leaves a foul taste in the predator's mouth.

Found in western Africa, hairy frogs will break their own toes to create claws. Scientists believe they do this when they feel threatened. The unusual sight of a frog producing cat-like claws has given them the name, "horror frogs".

Kaboom!

Termites found in French Guiana have blue crystals inside their stomach. When bitten by a predator, their stomach explodes and the blue crystals mix with their saliva to create a toxic blue liquid that kills both them and the predator.

Creature Feature!

HIPPOPOTAMUS

Hippos are semi-aquatic creatures that have an appetite to match their bulky appearance. They can eat an average of 35 kilograms (5.5 stone) of grass a night. Their diet means they produce a large amount of gas but, rather than being loud as you'd expect, their farts are generally silent.

Block it out

Hippos spend a huge amount of time in the water to stay out of the burning sun. When they are out of the water, hippos produce an oozing, red, oily liquid that both cools them and acts as a sunblock.

Grim spin

When hippos poo, their tails spin to spread the droppings as far as possible. The poo can be flung up to 10 metres (33 feet) – that's as long as a small bus. They do this to mark their territory.

Name:
Hippopotamus

Nickname: Hippo, River horse

Place of Origin:
Africa

Size: 3.3–5 metres (10.8–16.5 feet)

Danger! Danger!

Hippos are very aggressive and will use their huge, metre-long tusks to fight anything that threatens them, including humans. They are fast runners, reaching speeds of up to 31 kilometres (19 miles) per hour.

PESKY PARASITES

Parasites are living organisms that live on or in animals, including humans. The creatures that host the parasites are usually much larger than them. Some parasites spread disease, some cause pain, and some exist without the hosts even knowing they are there!

Green-banded broodsacs infect snail's eyes to look like caterpillars. When birds eat them the broodsacs can reproduce.

Web of lies

Your wish is my command.

Some parasitic female wasps will search for a suitable host after mating. This is usually an orb-weaving spider and the wasp will use its venom to take control of it. The venom paralyses the spider while the wasp glues her eggs to the spider's stomach. When the eggs hatch, the larvae release a chemical that makes the spider spin a completely new web. This web is a cocoon for the larvae and once it is complete, the larvae will kill and eat the spider.

The tongue-eating sea louse lives up to its name. The female of the species will attach itself to the base of a fish's tongue and suck on the blood, until the tongue dies and withers away. The louse will then take the place of the tongue and feed on the fish's blood or mucus. Strange as it may seem, the fish itself will not die and the two can live side by side for years.

Tick tock

Ticks are small arachnids (creepy-crawlies with eight legs) that do not jump or fly. To feed, they will usually wait on blades of grass before latching onto a host. Once there, they will burrow their head into the skin and feed for two to three days, sometimes doubling in size as they fill with blood.

TIME TO PEE PEE

Wee is made in the kidneys when water and waste is removed from the blood. It is then carried to the bladder where it is stored until it is time to go to the toilet. Some animals get rid of waste through small openings in their antennae – how strange!

Tuck in, kids!

Oh, rats!

Rats will wee on food they are eating. The wee will leave a scent that tells younger rats that the food is safe to eat.

Err... thanks?

Drop drop

Some smaller animals do not have enough liquid in their bodies to have a flow of wee. Instead, they deposit little drops.

Spray it with love

Rhinos wee backwards. Not only that, but instead of just weeing, they will sometimes spray it out to impress other rhinos. The spray can travel up to 4 metres (13 feet) – that's about the length of a car!

Glowing review

Cat wee glows in the dark. When placed under an ultraviolet light it shines brightly due to the high levels of the chemical phosphorus.

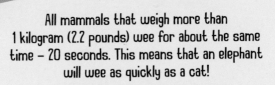

All mammals that weigh more than 1 kilogram (2.2 pounds) wee for about the same time – 20 seconds. This means that an elephant will wee as quickly as a cat!

SERIOUS SPITTERS

Spit, slobber, dribble – it all serves a purpose in the animal kingdom. While you may have stopped drooling when you were a baby, lots of animals use their saliva to help them clean, communicate, and even hunt.

Spraying cobras

Although their name may suggest otherwise, spitting cobras do not really spit. Instead, they spray their venom like a water gun. The venom is forced out through their hollow fangs and into the eyes of targets more than 2 metres (6.5 feet) away – that's the length of a giraffe's neck! But while a water fight with a snake might sound fun, knowing that the venom can cause possible blindness might make you think again.

It's a knockout!

Siamese archer fish squirt water to catch insects and small animals. The jet of water knocks their prey off plants or rocks, into the water below, where they are quickly eaten. Young archer fish learn this skill in groups which means one of them will always hit the target!

So embarrassing

Have you ever been embarrassed by your mum spitting into a tissue and cleaning your face? Baby kangaroos might know how you feel. Mother kangaroos spread their spit over the joeys to help them to cool down.

Enough, Mum!

Creature Feature!

KOMODO DRAGON

Found on five islands in Indonesia, Komodo dragons are the largest lizards on Earth. They are powerful creatures with scaly skin, short legs, and a long tail that is the same length as its body. These animals are fascinating, terrifying, and most definitely ghastly!

Chuck and run!

When threatened, Komodo dragons will vomit up the contents of their stomachs to make them faster at running.

Teeth like knives

Komodo dragons have 60 serrated teeth which means that each tooth has lots of sharp little points. This makes it easier for them to tear through the flesh and bones of prey.

Name: Komodo d[...]

Nickname: Buaya darat ("land crocodile")

Place of Origin: Indonesia

Size: 1.8–3 metres (6–10 feet)

Varied diet

Komodo dragons are carnivores and can eat much larger prey than themselves, such as buffalo and deer. They will also eat pigs, smaller dragons, and even humans.

PUTRID PETS

Cats, dogs, hamsters, fish, rabbits, even tarantulas – pets come in all shapes and sizes. They also come with a whole host of gross and ghastly habits that might make even the most loyal pet owner squirm!

Rabbits will sometimes eat their poo to gather extra nutrients from the partially digested food they ate the first time.

Hair raising

Cat owners have to deal with hairballs. These are made up of fur that cats swallow while grooming themselves. Some of these hairs will come out in the cat's poo but some will remain in the stomach. When the hairballs get too big, cats will vomit them up. Hairballs are usually around 2.5 centimetres (1 inch) long – that's slightly smaller than a paperclip. They are shaped like a sausage.

Unfussy eaters

Mmmm! Breakfast, lunch, and dinner!

Dogs will often eat their own vomit because they don't see it as vomit, just another source of food. Mother dogs often vomit up food to help the pups move from milk to solid food. Eating their own poop is also common, maybe because they are hungry, stressed, lacking nutrition, or simply because they like the taste. So the next time you let a dog lick your face, you may want to find out what it had for its last meal!

Teething problems

Hamsters are small pets that have thick, silky fur and short tails. Their teeth never stop growing and they usually grind them down by gnawing on food. They then need to be trimmed with special scissors. So if you think your parents are bad, nagging you to clean your teeth, imagine them asking you to snip them!

PROWLING PREDATORS

Predators are animals that hunt other animals. They are carnivores, meaning they eat other animals. They will usually eat herbivores (animals who eat only plants) but will also eat each other. Some ambush, some chase, but they'll all do whatever it takes to capture their prey!

Dance craze

Stoats are small mammals often found in woodlands and mountains. They have pointed faces, little ears, and are closely related to weasels. Their diet consists of small prey, like mice and voles, but they will also tackle prey much larger than themselves. To catch a rabbit, they will perform an energetic dance that hypnotizes the rabbit, and then pounce on them.

Ooh, ooh, aah, aah!

First impressions

Tigers are rumoured to use a sneaky trick to attack prey. Although we think of tigers growling, they will also mimic the noises of other animals, including deer and monkeys. It is possible that the animals will be lured in to investigate the noise, which then gives the tiger the chance to attack. And the tiger is so powerful that it can kill with just one swipe of a paw – SMACK!

Slimy prowler

The rosy wolfsnail from the United States is a fast-moving snail that attacks and eats other snails. Moving three times faster than other snails, the predator will sneak up behind their victim before eating them – sometimes shell and all.

Who's afraid of the big bad wolfsnail?

BAD LUCK BEASTS

Folklore and tales from all over the world have linked many species of animals to bad luck. One of the best known is that it's bad luck for a black cat to cross your path – although in Japan it's good luck!

Finger of death

Aye-ayes are lemurs that are native to Madagascar. They have an extra-long middle finger that they use for hunting grubs hidden within hollow branches. It has been called the "finger of death" and many people fear the consequences of the finger being pointed at them.

Pretty in pink

Pink dolphins can be found in the Amazon. Although born grey, they become pink as they age. Legend has it that these pink dolphins were once humans. To some, pink dolphins are sacred and it is bad luck to kill one.

Look at this cute photo from when you were little.

Mum! You're so embarrassing!

Murder at the window

In European legends, black crows are closely linked to death due to their menacing appearance and loud calls. Some associate the number of crows seen with having different meanings. Six crows are said to be the worst, as it is believed that death will follow. Their reputation may explain why a group of crows is known as a "murder".

Countdown to death

Ta dah!

Deathwatch beetles live in old trees or decaying wood. They're not much bigger than a grain of rice but can cause major damage to wooden furniture. Males will tap against dead wood to attract a mate and hearing this tapping is traditionally linked to bad luck.

Not all bad

Not all animals are said to bring bad luck. Other superstitions link black ants to increased wealth, frogs to good weather and, in ancient Egypt, beetles were bearers of good fortune.

This doesn't feel like good luck!

HELLBENDER SALAMANDER

Hellbender salamanders are amphibious carnivores that are covered in mucus. They have a flat head and body, four short, stubby legs, and a rudder-like tail, which means they are well-adapted to living in streams and rivers.

Skin breathers

Up until they are two years old, the salamander will breathe through gills. But once these disappear, the animals will breathe entirely through their skin. The creatures do have lungs, but these are used to help them float.

It won't grow back

Unlike other salamanders, hellbender salamanders are unable to regrow their limbs once they have been bitten off.

Name: Hellbender salamander

Nickname: Snot otter, Lasagne lizard, Devil dog, Mud-devil, Grampus, Mud-dog, Spotted water gecko

Place of Origin: USA

Size: 24–74 centimetres (9.5–29 inches)

Stand guard

The males take an active role in finding burrows in which females can lay their eggs. Once they have been deposited, the male will chase the female away and guard the eggs himself. However, despite standing guard over the eggs, he will also eat some. Once the eggs hatch, the larvae will quickly leave the burrow to avoid being eaten as well.

SO SICK!

Sick, puke, barf – vomit comes under many different names. While vomiting can help rid the body of harmful substances, animals also use vomit to defend themselves or even as a source of food. Now that's sick.

Projectile vomit

Turkey vultures will vomit on predators to help them escape, leaving a trail of burning, acidic sick on any attacker. They can launch the vomit up to 3 metres (10 feet), the height of a basketball hoop!

Baby barf

The babies of European rollers, small birds found in Africa, Asia, and Europe, will vomit a gross, orange liquid that deters predators. The smell of the vomit alerts the parents that their offspring have been scared by something and to approach the nest with caution.

Sweet story

Many people think that honey is made from bee vomit, but that's not quite true. After visiting a flower and collecting the sweet nectar, the bee will store the juice in their honey stomach – which is different to their stomach for food. When full, they travel back to the hive and pass the nectar from bee to bee using their mouths. Gradually the nectar will turn into honey.

Bee venom has been used for thousands of years as a way of treating certain illnesses!

The baby is being sick! Someone's here!

FESTERING FEEDERS

While you may have heard of the "five second rule", there are plenty of creatures that will tuck into rotting and decomposing food that has been left for days. Animals that eat decaying meat or plant matter are known as scavengers and include birds, mammals, and insects.

Mmmm, best for last!

Every last bit

Spotted hyenas are skilled hunters that can take down wildebeest, birds, lizards, and snakes. They are also efficient scavengers, helping themselves to any leftovers from other predators. Strong jaws and sharp teeth help hyenas to slice through thick meat and to easily grind down bone. They do not waste food and will eat almost every part of an animal's body, including the teeth.

Not all scavengers wait until their food is dead to start feasting. As well as munching on rotting carcasses, blowflies will feed on the cuts and grazes of healthy cattle, eating the dead flesh around the wound. They lay their eggs on dung or decaying flesh, which the maggots eat upon hatching.

Rotten reaper

Jackals are both predators and scavengers. They work in packs to take down small antelope, birds, and reptiles. However, their main source of food comes from scavenging animals killed by larger predators. Even though the flesh may have been decomposing for days, it won't stop the jackal tucking in. They will throw it up for their young offspring to eat, too.

PARROTFISH

The parrotfish name comes from their bird-like beaks that they use to scrape algae from coral reefs. Chunks of coral that are also ripped off from the reef, are ground down using their human-like teeth, digested, and then pooped out as sand. Scientists estimate that more than 80 per cent of the sand found around tropical coral reefs is made up of their poo!

Reef royalty

Species of parrotfish include the humphead, rainbow, stoplight, midnight, princess, and queen.

fishy dishy

Parrotfish are considered a delicacy in many parts of the world and, in Polynesia, were once considered "royal food" and only eaten by the king.

Name:
Parrotfish

Nickname:
Cattle of the sea

Place of Origin:
Atlantic, Indian, and Pacific Oceans

Size:
30–120 centimetres
(12–47 inches)

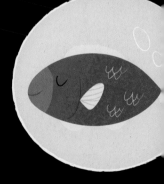

Bubble trouble

At night, some parrotfish hide in cracks in the reef and others bury themselves in the sand, but some build themselves a cocoon of mucus to rest in. The "bubble" has a bad smell and is thought to mask the scent of the parrotfish, so they are harder to find by predators. In the morning, the sleeping bag is thrown away.

THINGS THAT STING

Creatures that have stingers use them for two major reasons – to capture prey and to avoid being eaten. Insects, jellyfish, stingrays, and more – in the animal kingdom there are plenty of things that sting!

Burning up

Fire ants get their name from the burning sensation that is caused by their sting. Huge groups of fire ants can come together to overpower large animals such as turtles. They can be found in South America and North America, where they live in colonies of up to 200,000 ants.

No fairytail ending

Arizona bark scorpions are found in the south of the United States and northern Mexico. They hunt at night and feed on cockroaches, crickets, and spiders. Bark scorpions can control the amount of venom they inject depending on the size of their prey. They are good climbers, and are often found in trees. More worryingly, they are sometimes found under sinks, baths, and, cupboards in people's homes.

Hello. Nice sink!

Spiky spines

The most venomous fish in the world is the stonefish, found on the coasts of Australia. They have 13 spines along their backs, each armed with deadly venom. Masters of disguise, they are often mistaken for coral or stones and stepped on by mistake.

TARDIGRADES

Tardigrades are tiny, near-microscopic aquatic creatures that can be found in many habitats. They have short, squashy bodies and eight legs, with between four and eight claws on each. They are considered to be Earth's most indestructible animals.

Hot or cold

Tardigrades can stand freezing temperatures of -200 degrees Celsius (-328 degrees Fahrenheit) and up to the scorching heights of 148 degrees Celsius (298 degrees Fahrenheit). They can be boiled or frozen, and still live to tell the tale.

Weigh a tun

To survive extreme conditions, tardigrades pull in their arms and legs to turn into a little dehydrated ball called a tun. If put back into water they can wake up again within a few hours.

To infinity!

In 2007, scientists discovered that tardigrades can survive in outer space. For 10 days, the creatures endured radiation from the sun and the vacuum of outer space with no ill effects. There are also a number of tardigrades living on the moon after an Israeli spacecraft crash-landed with them on board in 2019.

Name:
Tardigrade

Nickname: Water bears, Moss piglets

Place of Origin:
Worldwide

Size: 0.1–1.2 millimetres (0.004–0.05 inches)

WHERE IN THE WORLD?

From the giant whale to the tiny ant, every continent is inhabited with a whole host of diverse creatures. Take a trip around the globe and meet some incredible animals!

Australia

Ghost bats are the only carnivorous bats to be found in Australia. They feed on frogs, birds, lizards, insects, and even other bats. They have pale grey fur and thin skin on their wings, which gives them a ghostly appearance.

Iran

The Iranian spider-tailed viper has a knobbly growth on its tail that looks like a spider. The snake will wiggle the "spider" to attract unsuspecting birds. When a bird swoops to try and eat the "spider", the snake will quickly strike.

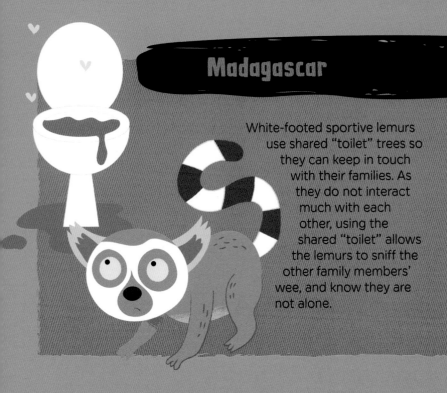

Madagascar

White-footed sportive lemurs use shared "toilet" trees so they can keep in touch with their families. As they do not interact much with each other, using the shared "toilet" allows the lemurs to sniff the other family members' wee, and know they are not alone.

Brazil

Kinkajous are carnivorous animals related to raccoons. They are also known as "honey bears" and are often found raiding beehives to satisfy their sweet tooth. They spend a lot of time in the trees and can turn their feet backwards to help them run up and down branches.

Hang on. Which way am I going again?

EYELASH PIT VIPER

Eyelash pit vipers get their name from the unique set of scales above their eyes that look like eyelashes. They can be found in many different colours but green and yellow are the most common. Their colour depends on their habitat, with green ones found near vegetation, and yellow ones near banana plantations. Some eyelash pit vipers have made a surprise appearance inside boxes of imported bananas. Yikes!

Dance-off!

When two males are looking for a mate, they will perform a dance in an attempt to intimidate each other.

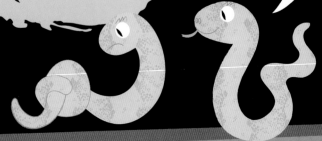

That's "knot" how you dance!

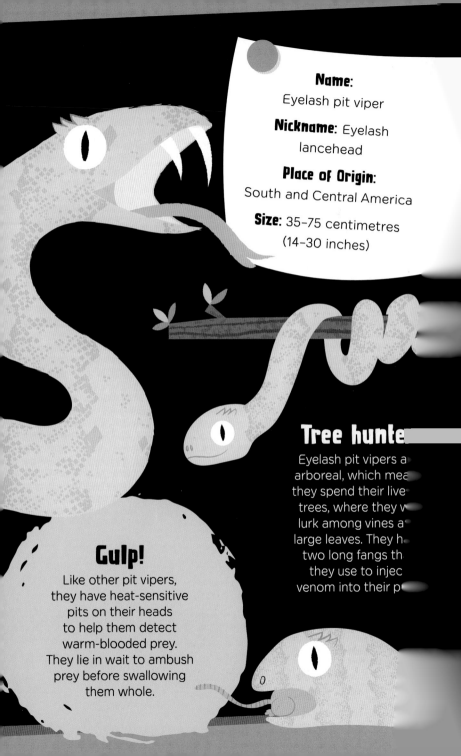

Name:
Eyelash pit viper

Nickname: Eyelash
lancehead

Place of Origin:
South and Central America

Size: 35–75 centimetres
(14–30 inches)

Tree hunte[r]

Eyelash pit vipers a[re]
arboreal, which mea[ns]
they spend their live[s in]
trees, where they w[ill]
lurk among vines a[nd]
large leaves. They h[ave]
two long fangs th[at]
they use to injec[t]
venom into their p[rey.]

Gulp!

Like other pit vipers,
they have heat-sensitive
pits on their heads
to help them detect
warm-blooded prey.
They lie in wait to ambush
prey before swallowing
them whole.

SHOCKING!

Animals use a variety of techniques to hunt, move, and survive, and some even use the power of electricity. On these pages, be prepared for some truly shocking behaviour!

Cool climbers

Geckos are known for their ability to climb walls and ceilings, but nobody really understands how they do it. While some think it could be due to the tiny hairs on a gecko's feet, new studies suggest it could also be down to static electricity.

Buzz kill

Stargazer fish eyes are on the tops of their heads. Behind the eyes is a special organ that can produce electric shocks if a predator tries to attack. They are also venomous, injecting toxins from two spines behind their eyelids if the unlucky predator gets too close.

Feel the force

Echidnas are mammals that come from mainland Australia, New Guinea, and Tasmania. They are covered in spines and have thin beaks. The skin of their beaks is very sensitive to the electric impulses given off from prey and this helps them to find food. Echidnas have no teeth but grind their food against the roof of their mouths using their spiky tongues.

Charge me up!

Electric rays, also known as torpedo fish, can grow over 1.8 metres (6 feet) in length and weigh more than 90 kilograms (200 pounds) – that's the same size as a big man! Their kidney-shaped organs store electricity like batteries. They will stun prey using their electricity and then use their fins to guide the victim towards their waiting mouths.

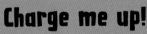

NIGHTY NIGHT

Animals that are active at night and sleep during the day are known as nocturnal. Some do this to avoid predators or to escape the heat of the sun, while others find hunting easier under the cover of darkness.

Night light

Fireflies are a type of beetle and there are more than 2,000 species of them – although not all species produce light. The light can be yellow, green, or orange, and is produced when air reacts with a chemical called luciferin. Flashing, pulsing, or flickering, the fireflies can put on quite the show!

Don't let the bedbugs bite!

As the old rhyme suggests, bedbugs like to bite humans. They are good at hiding during the day, before being tempted out at night, in part by the carbon dioxide in our breath. They are around the size of an apple seed and have flat bodies before feeding. They can suck up to seven times their own body weight in blood during a feed.

In a flap

There are more than 1,000 species of bat and they make up a fifth of the world's mammal population. They hunt in complete darkness, and use high-pitched sounds and echoes to locate prey.

It's a hoot

There are around 200 species of owl and most hunt small mammals, insects, and other small birds. Their large eyes and excellent hearing enable them to be efficient hunters in darkness and they use their powerful claws to catch and kill prey. Owls can see 10 times better than humans in the dark.

INTRODUCING...

Scientists discover new species of animal every year. Discoveries of new animals can help us to understand more about our world and how to protect the creatures that live in it. Here are some recent discoveries!

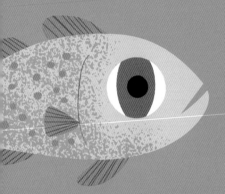

Cat eyes

Found in Papua New Guinea in 2019, the cat-eyed cardinalfish has similar eyes to a cat, with vertical pupils rather than round ones. They feed at night on plankton and small fish, and measure less than 2.5 centimetres (1 inch) in length.

A beetle named Yoda

Trigonopterus yoda is a species of flightless weevil, a type of beetle, named after Yoda from the *Star Wars* films, due to its bright green body. They were discovered in 2019 in the remote rainforests of Indonesia.

Green like Yoda I am.

Free ride

Yeehaw!

The hitchhiking beetle uses its strong jaws to hold on to the tummy of an ant. The beetle's colour and shape are similar to the ant's, which makes it difficult to detect. The beetle lives off the scraps from ant colonies. It was discovered in Costa Rica in 2017.

Although you'd think fire-tailed zogue zogues would be easy to spot, they are quite hard to see up in the treetops!

A fiery tail

Fire-tailed zogue zogues are primates that were discovered in the Amazon rainforest in 2011. Their name comes from their red tails that stand out against the grey fur of their bodies. They also have red patches of fur on their necks and sideburns.

YOU SUCK!

Hematophage is the name given to an animal that sucks blood as a source of food. While some are not fussy where they find it, some only feed on blood from particular parts of the body. Come and meet the real-life vampires!

Dracula ants get their name from the way they sometimes feed on the blood of their larvae.

World's deadliest

An encounter with a crocodile, shark, or lion isn't appealing but the title of "World's Deadliest" belongs to a much, much smaller creature. According to the WHO (World Health Organisation), mosquitoes are responsible for the deaths of more than 700,000 people each year, due to the diseases they spread. Female mosquitoes are the biters; they use the sharp tip of their straw-like mouth to pierce the skin and suck the blood.

Leeches are worms with segmented bodies that can live both on land and in water. They feed on the blood of a range of animals including fish, frogs, birds, and, if they can get it, humans. To keep the blood flowing, they release a special chemical that stops it from clotting. Leeches can suck several times their own body weight in blood in one sitting, tucking in for two to three hours before they are full!

Hey! You cut in!

Vampires going cheep!

Found on the Galápagos Islands, vampire finches will feed on the blood of larger birds, such as the blue-footed booby. They will pick at the tail feathers until there is a pool of blood that the finch can drink up. It is so popular that other finches will sit in a queue, patiently waiting until it's their turn to feed!

FUNNY NAMES!

Animals get their names from all manner of places. Some get their names from how they look, how they sound, and in some cases, how they taste!

Screaming hairy armadillo

Screaming hairy armadillos live in Argentina, Bolivia, and Paraguay, and are omnivorous (meaning they'll eat anything), feeding on plants, insects, and small vertebrates. Their name comes from the loud squealing noise they make if they are picked up.

Tasselled wobbegong

A type of shark, tasselled wobbegongs have fleshy beards and camouflaged skin, which means they can lay on the seabed waiting for their prey. The sharks attract prey by waving their tails. They can be found in the waters around northern Australia, Indonesia, and Papua New Guinea.

Red-lipped batfish

Despite being a fish, red-lipped batfish are not especially strong swimmers. Instead, they use their pectoral fins to "walk" along the ocean floor. Although their bodies are light brown and greyish, their bright red lips make them stand out from the crowd.

Chicken turtle

Cluck!

Found in the south-eastern United States, chicken turtles have long necks and brown shells streaked with yellow lines. The name comes from their flesh, which is said to taste like chicken.

On the menu

Some animals are named after their resemblance to foods. These include the ice cream cone worm, fried egg jellyfish, chocolate chip sea stars, and pineapplefish.

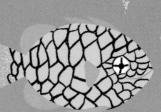

SALTWATER CROCODILE

The largest species of crocodile, "salties" are equipped with 66 sharp teeth that they use to devour prey, such as water buffalo, monkeys, boar, and sometimes even humans. They are explosive hunters, thrashing and grabbing their victims before drowning them in the water.

Speedy swimmers

Using their huge tails, saltwater crocodiles can reach speeds of up to 29 kilometres per hour (18 miles per hour) – that's faster than most sailboats!

Surf's up!

Saltwater crocodiles can be found in the open sea. They use the currents of the oceans to travel to different islands. Scientists tracked some crocodiles who had travelled over 250 miles (402 kilometres) in just 19 days.

Name:
Saltwater crocodile

Nickname: Salties,
Sea crocodile

Place of Origin:
Eastern India, southeast Asia,
and northern Australia

Size: 5–7 metres
(17–23 feet)

Mega bites!

Saltwater crocodile bites
are the strongest in the
animal kingdom and are
powerful enough to
crush bone.

REGENERATORS

Animals will do whatever it takes to survive, and some will even risk life and limb – literally. Dropping tails and losing legs can help some animals escape from predators, and many have the ability to grow back the lost parts of their body.

Half-time

Starfish can regrow limbs that have been eaten by predators. Some species can even break themselves in half and regrow the limbs to create two new starfish.

Flip out!

Squid will somersault to snap off their limbs if they have been captured by a predator. They are also prepared to lose a limb before they are captured, hooking their arms onto their attacker before propelling themselves away, leaving some of the limbs behind.

Snack attack

Found throughout northern Africa, spiny mice get their name from the stiff hairs on their backs – similar to a hedgehog's spines. They have skin that is easily torn, which helps them escape from predators. When caught or bitten, they drop patches of their skin to escape, while the attacker tucks into a flaky snack.

Spiny mice have a varied diet that includes seeds, nuts, fruit, insects, and rotting meat.

See ya!

MURKY MONSTERS

If one batch of creepy critters wasn't enough, here's another group of spooky-sounding animals that can be found all over the world!

Halloween pennant

Halloween pennants are a species of dragonfly found in the United States. They get their name from their yellow-orange wings, which are patterned with dark stripes. Like most dragonflies, they live near water and feed on small insects that they capture while flying.

Ghost ant

Ghost ants have a dark head with a pale stomach and legs. They are very small and are considered annoying because they spread germs. They are also known as "sugar ants" due to their love of sweet food.

Coffin ray

Native to Australian waters, coffin rays have enormous mouths, allowing them to gulp down prey half the size of their bodies. Although crabs and fish are their usual diet, a dead ray was once found with a penguin in it's stomach! They can also deliver powerful electric shocks.

Skeleton shrimp

With their bony, stick-like bodies, skeleton shrimp are tiny creatures that are just a few millimetres in length. Their pale colouring allows them to camouflage against the vegetation on the sea floor. They have powerful claws that they use for defending, grooming, and feeding. After mating, however, some females may also use their claws to kill males by injecting them with venom.

FILTHY FLIES

Flies live in every part of the world apart from Antarctica. While they can be disgusting, they help pollinate plants and get rid of decaying animals. With more than 120,000 species of fly, here is just a small selection!

Rotten reproducers

Flies are not fussy where they lay their eggs and will happily plop them onto poo, sludge, and rotting flesh. This gives the larvae a ready-made meal to tuck into when they turn into maggots.

Keep your head

Fruit flies can survive without heads. Scientists have observed the headless creatures grooming themselves, walking, and even flying. Although they can be annoying, your supply of chocolate would be in trouble without fruit flies, because they pollinate the flowers of the cacao tree.

Flies do not have teeth. Instead they have a long tongue called a proboscis, which they use like a straw to suck up food. They will vomit onto their meal, too. The acid dissolves the food and makes it easier to slurp up.

Cycle of life

Botflies are hairier and larger than house flies. They lay eggs on a range of mammals. Once the eggs hatch, the larvae will either burrow into the host's skin or crawl into the mouth or nose. Once they're big enough, the larvae will fall onto the ground, ready to turn into new botflies.

EPIC YUCK!

Spit, pee, and slime might not sound appetizing, but on this page they're the recipe for success! Here are some more facts to make you say, "Yuck!"

Hedgegobs!

Despite being covered in sharp spines, hedgehogs will also spread spit onto their quills. After chewing poisonous toads and plants, the hedgehog's spit becomes extra bubbly. They will then use their tongues and paws to spread the spit.

Mouth of wee!

Many animals give out a foul odour when threatened and the Chinese softshell turtle is one of these, producing a fluid from the edge of its shell. However, what makes this creature stand out from other stinky animals is how it gets rid of its pee. While most animals wee out of their backsides, Chinese softshell turtles wee out of their mouths.

Super slime!

When you think of slimy animals, slugs must surely be near the top of the list. Slugs use slime to move and, because it's sticky, to climb up walls and windows. It also helps the slug anchor itself to avoid being picked off by a predator. When a slug finds a safe place to rest, chemicals in its slimy trail can help it find its way back after searching for food.

Spit it out

Llamas have a reputation for being spitters. They spit to stop others from eating their food, when threatened by a predator, or when showing other llamas in the group who is in charge.

I LOVE EWW!

What do animals do when they're looking for a mate? In the animal kingdom, it isn't always sunsets and roses – sometimes it's love at first bite!

Sweet perfume

Male koalas have scent glands in the centres of their chests that produce a dark, sticky goo. The koalas will rub this smelly goo on trees to mark out their territory. More than 35 chemicals make up the scent and it's at its smelliest in the spring – when they are trying to attract a mate.

Dance of death

Female jumping spiders make harsh judges. If males do not impress the females with their dancing, they may well end up as dinner.

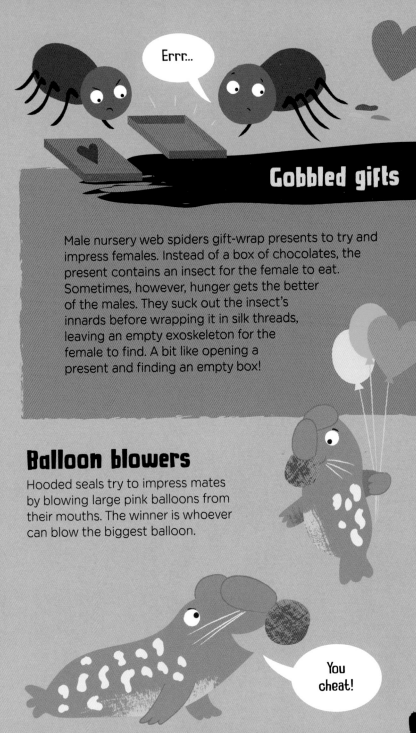

Errr...

Gobbled gifts

Male nursery web spiders gift-wrap presents to try and impress females. Instead of a box of chocolates, the present contains an insect for the female to eat. Sometimes, however, hunger gets the better of the males. They suck out the insect's innards before wrapping it in silk threads, leaving an empty exoskeleton for the female to find. A bit like opening a present and finding an empty box!

Balloon blowers

Hooded seals try to impress mates by blowing large pink balloons from their mouths. The winner is whoever can blow the biggest balloon.

You cheat!

GROSS OUT!

Animals get up to some pretty gross behaviour in every part of their lives. From passing gas to clearing their nose, there's plenty of yucky facts to find!

World beaters

Termites fart more than any other animal on the planet. These tiny insects are believed to be part of the problem of global warming, due to the levels of methane they produce. Apart from farting, they will also eat each other's poo, and they even use poo to build their homes.

Aw, Mum!

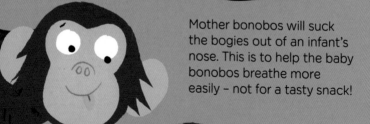

Mother bonobos will suck the bogies out of an infant's nose. This is to help the baby bonobos breathe more easily – not for a tasty snack!

Gross.

Time to poo!

Researchers have found that all animals, no matter how big or small, take around the same amount of time to poo. The magic number? 12 seconds. It's thought that if they take any longer, they may be attacked by predators who like the smell of their poo.

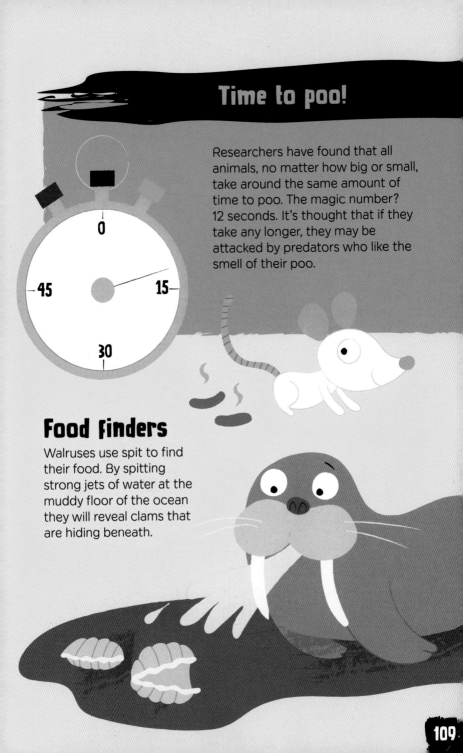

Food finders

Walruses use spit to find their food. By spitting strong jets of water at the muddy floor of the ocean they will reveal clams that are hiding beneath.

MATCH THE ANIMAL TO THE POO

Animal poo comes in all different shapes, sizes, and smells. Using your finger, can you match the animals to their droppings? Check the answers on page 121.

1

2

3

4

A

B

C

D

ANIMAL SILHOUETTES

Match the animal names to their silhouettes, using your finger. Or will you be kept in the dark?

1

2

3

4

5

6

A **Cassowary**

B **Tick**

C **Hagfish**

D **Yeti crab**

E **Draco lizard**

F **Aye-aye**

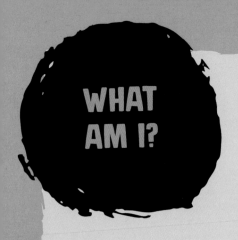

WHAT AM I?

Use the facts to find out which three animals are being described. How many clues did it take for you to work it out?

1
1. I can run 31 kilometres (19 miles) per hour.
2. I spend a lot of time in water to stay out of the sun.
3. When I poo, my tail spins around to fling it away.
4. I have tusks that measure 1 metre (3.3 feet) long.
5. One of my nicknames is "river horse".

2
1. When I feed, it takes two to three hours before I feel full.
2. I release a special chemical that stops blood from clotting.
3. I am a worm that can live on land or in water.
4. I can eat several times my own body weight in one go.
5. I feed on the blood from a range of animals.

3
1. I live in tropical forests.
2. I am a type of bird that lives in southeast Asia and Australia.
3. I am the most deadly bird to humans.
4. I am a large bird with sharp claws.
5. I have a kick powerful enough to kill a human.

These rats have got themselves into quite the tangle. Using your finger can you find out who each tail belongs to before they knot themselves up?!

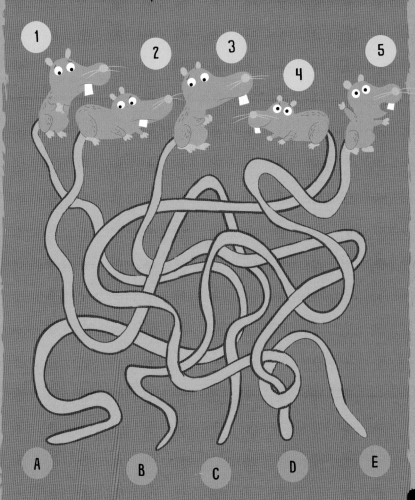

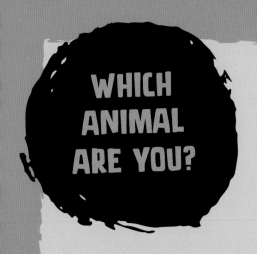

WHICH ANIMAL ARE YOU?

Answer all the questions to find out which animal you are most similar to!

1 Which best describes your appetite?

A Feed me now!

B I have enough food around me so I can eat when I need to.

C I don't eat often. If I skip a meal, I'll hardly notice.

D I like to graze on food throughout the day.

2 Which of these is your favourite?

A A mix of meat and vegetables.

B Juice

C Meat

d Veggies

3 Where do you like to hang out?

A Out in the open where I can roam free.

B Somewhere mucky.

C In the dark.

D Somewhere muddy.

4 Where would be your
ideal holiday?

A   South Africa

B   Egypt

C   Italy

D   America

5 How social do you like to be?

A   I'm always with my mates.

B   I like to be with a small group of close friends.

C   I'm happiest on my own.

D   I am happy being on my own but I
also like to meet up with friends.

ANSWERS

Mostly Ds
You are a capybara!

Mostly Cs
You are an olm!

Mostly Bs
You are a dung beetle!

Mostly As
You are a honey badger!

SPOT THE DIFFERENCE

Can you spot the 10 differences between these pictures? Use your finger to point them out!

TRUE OR FALSE?

1 Hoatzins, or "stink birds", smell like dog poo.

2 A poison dart frog has enough poison to kill 10 people.

3 There are only 10 species of bat.

4 Cockroaches cannot die.

5 Wombat poo is cube-shaped.

117

MANKY MAZE

This poor dung beetle can't remember where it has buried its poo. Can you help it find a way through the maze of tunnels, using your finger to follow the path, back to the delicious prize?

Now that you have learned all about the gross and ghastly facts, it's time to see what you know. Bring it on!

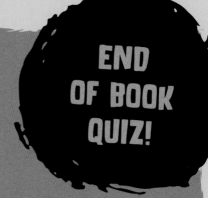

END OF BOOK QUIZ!

1 Which animal can be boiled or frozen, and live to tell the tale?
   A Zebras
   B Assassin bugs
   C Tardigrades
   D Lemurs

2 What type of animal is a "snot otter"?
   A Snake
   B Salamander
   C Otter
   D Bird

3 When vultures are too heavy to fly, what do they do to help?
   A Poo on their feet
   B Run instead
   C Hitch a ride on an elephant
   D Throw up

4 What do greater short-horned lizards squirt from their eyes to frighten predators?
   A Blood
   B Wee
   C Poo
   D Poison

5 Which animal is the "World's Deadliest"?
   A Lion
   B Great white shark
   C Blue-ringed octopus
   D Mosquito

NOW IT'S YOUR TURN!

Use your own research to create your very own fact page about a gross animal of your choice.

Grab a piece of paper and draw a picture. Then write one or two facts about it underneath.

Remember – the grosser the better!

Name: What's the name of your animal?

Other names: Does it have any nicknames?

Place of Origin: Where does it live?

Size: How big is it?

ANSWERS

Match the animal to the poo

1=C, 2=A, 3=D, 4=B

Animal silhouettes

1=B, 2=A, 3=D, 4=E, 5=C 6=F

What am I?

1 = Hippo, 2 = Leech,
3 = Cassowary

Find the correct tail

1=A, 2=C, 3=D, 4=E, 5=B

Spot the difference

True or false?

1 = FALSE! They smell like
cow manure.

2 = TRUE! Hunters used to
use it for their arrows.

3 = FALSE! There are
actually over 1,000 species!

4 = FALSE! They can survive
for weeks but will die
eventually.

5 = TRUE! They are the only
animals in the world to
do so.

Manky Maze

End of book quiz!

1 = C, Tardigrades

2 = B, Salamander

3 = D, Throw Up

4 = A, Blood

5 = B, Blobfish

GLOSSARY

adapted
How an animal has evolved over time to be better suited to its habitat

amphibians
Animals that start their life in water but can live both in water and on land. Most have moist skin

bacteria
Tiny living things

chemicals
Substance that is made when two or more substances react

colony
Group of animals that live together

crustaceans
Animals with a hard outer shell and jointed legs. They usually live in the water

echinoderms
Group of animals that don't have a backbone and live in the sea

fatal
Can cause death

fungus
Group of living things that includes mushrooms, toadstools and mould

gland
Sac inside an animal that produces special chemicals

larvae
Young of certain animals, including insects and amphibians, after they hatch from an egg

lethal
Something that can kill

mammals
Animals that have hair or fur, a backbone, and produce milk to feed their young

membrane
Thin piece of skin

mucus
Thick, slimy fluid

nutrients
Types of food that animals
need to survive

organism
Living thing, such as an
animal or plant

paralyzed
Unable to move

parasite
Animal that lives and feeds
on a bigger animal

poison
Chemical that causes harm
or death

predator
Animal that hunts other
animals for food

prey
Animal that is hunted and
eaten by another animal

primates
Group of animals that
includes monkeys

protein
Substance found in food
that helps bodies to grow

reptiles
Animals that have dry, scaly
skin and a backbone

regurgitate
When swallowed food is
brought back out of the
stomach to chew it again
or feed to someone else

spores
Cells that spread a fungus

toxins
Dangerous chemicals

venom
Poisonous liquid

vocal sac
Skin found on the throats
of amphibians which is used
to make sounds louder

INDEX

DK | Penguin Random House

Produced for DK by Collaborate Agency
Author and Illustrator Kev Payne

Consultant Dr Nick Crumpton

Editor Abi Luscombe
Senior Art Editor Elle Ward
Managing Editor Laura Gilbert
Jacket Co-ordinator Isobel Walsh
Publishing Manager Francesca Young
Senior Production Editor Rob Dunn
Senior Production Controller Inderjit Bhullar
Deputy Art Director Mabel Chan
Publishing Director Sarah Larter

First published in Great Britain in 2021
by Dorling Kindersley Limited
One Embassy Gardens, 8 Viaduct Gardens,
London, SW11 7AY

A CIP catalogue record for this book
is available from the British Library.
ISBN: 978-0-2415-0350-8

Printed and bound in China

For the curious
www.dk.com

MIX
Paper from
responsible sources
FSC™ C018179

This book was made with
Forest Stewardship Council ™
certified paper – one small step in DK's
commitment to a sustainable future.

For more information go to
www.dk.com/our-green-pledge

For my Mum, who gave me a love of
books and animals, even if they can
be Gross and Ghastly!

Special thanks also to Kate for
making this happen.

~ K.P.